The Wells of Our Fathers:

Hymn Study Workbook 1, Level 2

Written by Phil Routszong

Illustrated by Jennifer Routszong

Deep Calls Publishing

Havelock, NC

The Wells of Our Fathers: Hymn Study Workbook 1, Level 2

Copyright © 2013 by Phil Routszong, Jennifer Routszong

978-0-578-12481-0

TABLE OF CONTENTS

Weeks 1 and 2: Fanny Crosby – ***To God be the Glory***   1

Weeks 3 and 4: Reginald Heber – ***Holy, Holy, Holy***   9

Weeks 5 and 6: Frederick William Faber – ***Faith of Our Fathers***   17

Weeks 7 and 8: Henry Francis Lyte – ***Abide With Me***   25

Weeks 9 and 10: Joseph Hart – ***Come, Ye Sinners, Poor and Needy***   33

Weeks 11 and 12: George Croly – ***Spirit of God, Descend Upon My Heart***   41

Weeks 13 and 14: Bernard of Clairvaux – ***Jesus, the Very Thought of Thee***   49

Weeks 15 and 16: Edward Perronet – ***All Hail the Power of Jesus' Name***   57

Weeks 17 and 18: Samuel Stone – ***The Church's One Foundation***   65

Weeks 19 and 20: William Williams – ***Guide Me O Thou Great Jehovah***   73

Weeks 21 and 22: Christina Rossetti – ***None Other Lamb***   81

Weeks 23 and 24: William Kethe – ***All People That on Earth Do Dwell***   89

Introduction

So often, the true value of an object is only understood through the lens of time. We take a quick glance and make an initial judgment only to shrug off any feelings of the "what if". This is true for so many people concerning hymnody, especially children. The language of hymns can be intimidating, confusing and boring. The eternal truths they present are indeed treasure but that treasure is hidden in a field. We must dig for it. In this study, that digging is presented as a most worthy adventure. I have tried from the beginning to marry the language of hymns with the language of Scripture. The greatest hymns find their depths in the fountainhead of the Word of God. There can be no higher quest than the memorization of Scripture. It is how God's children are rooted and grounded in love. It is how we know the commands of Jesus, and are compelled and disciplined into the joys of obedience. We must give ourselves entirely to it, as we are training for eternity now. I owe a great deal of my Christian stability to the singing of hymns and to the mother and father that taught me the melodies.

As you venture from peak to peak, from glory to glory, pray that God would make the song real in your heart. Constantly ask the Father, "Am I singing a lie to You?" That is perhaps the hardest thing but the most necessary. Listen to Jesus preach to you through the words of the hymns and this study. Come every day seeking to know Him and be changed. It is only the changed life that can truly make Him known to the world.

Finally, allow the stories of the people in this book to encourage you. Begin to see that these people had one thing in common: they wanted to live for Jesus with no limits. There is not one task in this life that is too difficult for you should the Lord lead you to it. Never believe anyone if they tell you that you have to wait to live in glory with Jesus. If you are God's child, your life can be glorious now because of His presence. It is but the tiniest taste of heaven and it leaves you wanting more. Use this book as a tool to seek the presence of God. He is what makes heaven wonderful beyond description. As you live growing up in the presence of God, you will see what your life really is: a gift for His glory. Have fun on your adventure!

Come now, a little further down the road –

Phil

Fanny Crosby (1820-1915)
To God Be the Glory

To God be the glory, great things He hath done!
So loved He the world that He gave us his Son,
Who yielded His life an atonement for sin,
And opened the life-gate that we may go in.

Refrain:
Praise the Lord, praise the Lord,
Let the earth hear his voice!
Praise the Lord, praise the Lord,
Let the people rejoice!
O come to the Father thru Jesus the Son,
And give Him the glory, great things He hath done!

O perfect redemption, the purchase of blood,
To every believer the promise of God;
The vilest offender who truly believes,
That moment from Jesus a pardon receives.

Great things He hath taught us, great things He hath done,
And great our rejoicing thru Jesus the Son;
But purer, and higher, and greater will be
Our wonder, our transport, when Jesus we see.

To God be the Glory
Fanny Crosby (1820-1915)

"When I get to heaven, the first face that shall ever gladden my sight will be that of my Savior."

Does beauty speak to you? Do you often find the delight of God on any of your adventures? When you hear beautiful music, what do you think it is trying to say? When you are outside playing, do you hear the colors of nature singing the praises of God? Perhaps you never have noticed any of these things, but perhaps you soon will! The delight of our great God is all around us. We just have to stop what we are doing, and search for it.

Fanny Crosby loved every opportunity to find the delight of God. When she was a baby, she became ill. A man pretending to be a doctor prescribed the wrong treatment for her, and she became blind for the rest of her life. Fanny's father died just a few months later, and her mother had to work to support the family. Fanny soon found herself growing up with her grandmother.

Perhaps you have a different family than that of your friends. Perhaps God has led your life in a way that you did not expect. Yet even in every circumstance, Jesus is there! When you begin to wish that your life were different in some way, remember that it is a gift from Him. What will you choose to do with it?

Fanny believed with all of her heart that Jesus was always with her, even in her blindness. She refused to complain about her life. Instead, she would focus on the goodness of God! She would memorize five chapters of the Bible a week. Fanny would write poetry and hymns. She wrote over nine thousand hymns! Can you just imagine? God even gave her a husband who was one of New York City's best organists. He wrote the music for many of her hymns. Many times, musicians would stop by her home for hymn lyrics to tunes they had just written. One such musician was a man named William Doane. He needed lyrics quickly! His train was going to leave in thirty-five minutes. "Play me the tune!" Fanny said. As she listened, the music spoke to her. "Your music says 'Safe in the Arms of Jesus,'" said Fanny as she quickly wrote the words. "Read it on the train and hurry. You do not want to be late!" That hymn became one of Fanny's most famous.

If you are child of God, you do not need to wait for Sunday to worship Him. You must learn to look for His delight all around you. That is really what being His child is all about. You must learn to be happy in what makes Him happy. Seek out what gives your heavenly Father joy. You should probably start where Fanny did, in the wonderful Word of God. As you memorize it, ask God to show you just where His delight can be found. The writer of Hebrews wrote that God rewards those who diligently seek Him. Where will you find the delight of God today?

Week 1

Scripture Memory Work: Old Testament

"Thy word have I hid in mine heart, that I might not sin against thee."

-Psalm 119:11 (KJV)

Using a Merriam-Webster dictionary resource, define the following terms:

Glory: (*noun*)

1a._____

_____

1b._____

_____

2a._____

2b._____

3a._____

3b._____

Atonement: (*noun*)

1.*obsolete:*_____

2._____

_____

Reconcile: (*transitive verb*)

1a._____

1b._____

Redeem: (*transitive verb*)

1a._____

1b._____

2a._____

_____

2b._____

_____

2c._____

2d._____

Scripture Study – Psalm 119:1-11

Psalm 119 is the longest chapter in the entire Bible. Every verse speaks about the Word of God, but uses different words to describe it. Look for words like "way", "law", "statute", "commandment" or "judgment" as they are all used to describe God's Word.

1. In verses 1 & 2, what word describes people who love God's Word?

2. According to verse 2, how are we to seek God?

3. What do you think it means to seek God "with your whole heart"?

4. Verse 4 speaks of keeping God's law diligently? What does "diligently" mean?

5. According to verse 6, what does God's Word keep from us?

6. According to verse 7, what happens in our hearts when we learn God's Word?

7. In verse 9, how does a young person keep themselves pure?

8. What is the writer's prayer in verse 10?

9. According to verse 11, why should we memorize the Bible?

10. Have you already memorized some verses of the Bible? If so, please write one of your favorite verses from memory:

11. Based on your studies this week, what questions do you have for your parents? Please write them on page 8.

Week 2

Scripture Memory Work: New Testament

"Rejoice in the Lord always: and again I say, Rejoice."

-Philippians 4:4 (KJV)

Using a Merriam-Webster dictionary resource, define the following terms:

Rejoice: (*verb*)

transitive:

1._____

intransitive:

1._____

Pardon: (*noun*)

1._____

2._____

3a._____

3b._____

4._____

Vile: (*adjective*)

1a._____

1b._____

2._____

3._____

4._____

Transport: (*noun*)

1._____

2._____

3a._____

3b._____

4._____

Scripture Study – Philippians 4:4-8

The New Testament is filled with letters to churches, many of which were written by the Apostle Paul. In this week's study, explore the book of Philippians as you are able. Look for other instructions that God gave the church, and that He gives to you as well!

1. According to verse 4, when are God's children to rejoice in Him?

2. Given the definition of the word "rejoice", is it always a natural response of our hearts?

3. How can our hearts rejoice even in the middle of trouble? Who should make our hearts glad?

4. In verse 5, why should we let our moderation (other versions say "gentleness") be known unto all men?

5. According to verse 6, should we be anxious for anything? What should we do instead of worrying?

6. What is promised to keep our hearts and minds in verse 7?

7. According to verse 8, what are the things we should think about? Please list them below:

8. Based on your studies this week, what questions do you have for your parents? Please write them on page 8.

Questions for Parents:

Reginald Heber (1783 – 1826)
Holy, Holy, Holy

Holy, holy, holy! Lord God Almighty!
Early in the morning our song shall rise to Thee;
Holy, holy, holy, merciful and mighty!
God in three Persons, blessed Trinity!

Holy, holy, holy! All the saints adore Thee,
Casting down their golden crowns around the glassy sea;
Cherubim and seraphim falling down before Thee,
Who was, and is, and evermore shall be.

Holy, holy, holy! Though the darkness hide Thee,
Though the eye of sinful man Thy glory may not see;
Only Thou art holy; there is none beside Thee,
Perfect in pow'r, in love, and purity.

Holy, holy, holy! Lord God Almighty!
All Thy works shall praise Thy Name, in earth, and sky, and sea;
Holy, holy, holy; merciful and mighty!
God in three Persons, blessed Trinity!

Holy, Holy, Holy

Reginald Heber (1783-1826)

*"Only Thou art holy! There is **none** beside Thee!"*

Have you ever noticed just how different people are from one another? Even among your own family members, you are a completely different person than perhaps your sister, brother, mother or father. It is in our differences that we find just how much we are uniquely formed and shaped by God! Yet with all the variety of people here on the earth, God is a Person that is so unique that He alone possesses a word to describe the degree of His "uniqueness". That word is HOLY. I am quite sure that in your worship gatherings you have heard or even have said this word used to describe God. To say that God is holy means that He is nothing like us. He is "completely other than" us. God has revealed Himself as holy in the Bible, and has shown Himself to be holy countless times to millions of people in human history.

Reginald Heber was a poet in his childhood. Reginald was blessed to be reared in a family that put a high value on education, just like you! He became very good at translating Latin into English. He loved poetry. He would write poetry all the time. He loved how it would flow in meter and rhyme from the pens of masters like Lord Byron and Sir Walter Scott. Their stories would stoke the fires of Reginald's imagination. Reginald's poetry would win literary awards when he was just seven years old. (Never allow anyone to tell you that you are too young to do great things for God!) Reginald's family taught him about the love of Jesus. When he grew older, Reginald would study to be a pastor and would share Jesus' love with people in England for part of his life. He would write hymns that would try to help explain the complexities of God's character. In the last years of his life, Reginald would take his family to India to share Jesus' love in some of the most remote parts of that nation.

So what does the word "holy" mean? One of the meanings of "holy" is "sinless" or "completely pure". God cannot sin. Sin cannot exist in the pure presence of God. That is why God is a Person "completely other" than us. All we know is sin and its horrible effects on the world in which we live. When the Bible speaks of God's holiness, it speaks of that part of His nature in which every other part is completely bathed. God is holy in His power. God is holy in His love. God is holy in His knowledge. God is holy in His wrath. Everything God does is right and righteous, because everything God **IS** is right and righteous. It is a hard thought to think about sometimes, but we must think on God's holiness as often as we can. The holiness of God changes everything in our lives if we make it our focus. It changes the way we speak to one another. It changes the way we follow Jesus' (and our parents') commandments. It changes the way we think about our lives and our future. It helps us to see just how much we need Jesus to save every part of us.

Week 3

Scripture Memory Work: Old Testament

"Above it stood the seraphim: each one had six wings; with twain he covered his face, and with twain he covered his feet, and with twain he did fly. And one cried unto another, and said, Holy, holy, holy, is the Lord of hosts: the whole earth is full of his glory."

-Isaiah 6:2-3 (KJV)

Using a Merriam-Webster dictionary resource, define the following terms:

Seraphim: (*noun plural*)

1._____

2._____

_____

Merciful: (*adjective*)

1._____

Blessed: (*adjective*)

1a._____

1b._____

1c._____

2._____

_____

Trinity: (*noun*)

1._____

_____

2.*not capitalized:*_____

3._____

_____

Holy: (*adjective*)

1._____

_____

3._____

4a._____

4b._____

Scripture Study: Isaiah 6:1-8

1. Who is telling the story of this vision?

2. In what year did the vision occur?

3. Where was the LORD in the vision?

4. According to verse 2, how did the seraphim use their wings?

5. Why do you think they covered their face?

6. Why do you think they covered their feet?

7. In English, we use suffixes to mark differences in words. (i.e. "dirty, dirtier, dirtiest") In other languages they repeat the same word multiple times. Based on this fact, why do you think the seraphim used the word "Holy" three times in verse 3?

8. According to verse 4, what happened to the temple?

9. In verse 5, what was Isaiah's response to seeing God?

10. Why did Isaiah respond in such a way?

11. What did the seraph do in verses 6 & 7?

12. According to verse 8, what was Isaiah's heart attitude after seeing the Lord in all His glory?

13. Based on your studies this week, what questions do you have for your parents? Please write them on page 16.

Week 4

Scripture Memory Work: New Testament

"The four and twenty elders fall down before him that sat on the throne, and worship him that liveth for ever and ever, and cast their crowns before the throne, saying, Thou art worthy, O Lord, to receive glory and honor and power: for thou hast created all things, and for thy pleasure they are and were created."

-Revelation 4:10-11 (KJV)

Using a Merriam-Webster dictionary resource, define the following terms:

Sovereignty: (*noun*)
1._____
2a._____
2b._____
2c._____
3._____

Transcendent: (*adjective*)
1a._____
1b._____
2._____
3._____

Pure: (*adjective*)
1a.(1)_____(2)_____
_____(3)_____
2a._____
3a.(1)_____
(2):_____
3b._____

Immanent: (*adjective*)
1._____
2._____

Scripture Study: Revelation 4:8-11

The book of Revelation, written by the apostle John, was sent to all the churches in Asia Minor. It is full of word pictures and very descriptive language. If you read something you do not fully understand, you should ask your parents for help.

1. Name two things that are similar about this passage that you also found in the Isaiah passage from last week:

    1._____

    2._____

2. What do the elders do in verse 10?

3. Why do they cast their crowns before the throne?

4. According to verse 8, does this worship ever cease?

5. According to verse 11, what is the reason given for the glory of God?

6. Why were all things created?

7. Based on your studies this week, what questions do you have for your parents? Please write them on page 16.

Questions for Parents:

Frederick William Faber (1814 – 1863)
Faith of Our Fathers

Refrain:

Faith of our fathers, holy faith!
We will be true to thee till death.

Faith of our fathers, living still,
In spite of dungeon, fire and sword;
O how our hearts beat high with joy
Whenever we hear that glorious Word!

Faith of our fathers, we will strive
To win all nations unto Thee;
And through the truth that comes from God,
We all shall then be truly free.

Faith of our fathers, we will love
Both friend and foe in all our strife;
And preach Thee, too, as love knows how
By kindly words and virtuous life.

Faith of Our Fathers

Frederick William Faber (1814-1863)

"The music of the Gospel leads us home."

Do you sometimes find it difficult to behave the same way all the time? Do you change the way you behave or speak depending on who is around you? To your mom and dad you are one person, and around your friends you may be a completely different person. The reason for your difficulty is your original sinful nature. Yet even when we change, Jesus never does. God is always the same; He never changes. This part of His character is called *immutability*. Part of the work that God has promised to do in His children is to make them more consistent in their life's love for Him.

Frederick William Faber had to face such inconsistency. He not only dealt with himself, but also the lives of many members of his church. They would act like they loved Jesus on Sunday while being complete strangers to Him during the week. The Bible calls this behavior "hypocrisy" and if you are breathing right now, you live with it. There has only been one Person Who has lived on earth Who was not a hypocrite - the God-man Jesus Christ.

So what do you think Pastor Frederick did with the hypocrites? He followed Jesus in loving them. He would preach the high value of Jesus' worth. He would call people to repent, to hate their sin and love Jesus. In turn, the Spirit of God would work in people's hearts, just like He works in your heart if you are His child. The Bible says that the love of God brings people to repent and trust in Him.

Frederick would love to spend time outdoors. He would take long walks in the country, and more often than not the beauty of creation would inspire him to write poetry. He had a very friendly personality, but Frederick, like all of us, would need Jesus for consistency in his life.

That is the beauty of the gospel of Jesus. He knows that we cannot do anything for ourselves in light of eternity, yet He stands to make atonement for all that the Father has given Him. Even when we are faithless, even when we are inconsistent, He is faithful to His children for He cannot deny Himself. His faithfulness to us should stir our hearts to faithfulness to Him. His love for us should drive our hearts to love Him all the more. Do you sometimes find it difficult to be the same person all the time? Love Jesus with everything you are. You should continue loving Jesus because He first loved you. He has promised to work in the hearts of His children, and He Who promised is faithful.

Week 5

Scripture Memory Work: Old Testament

"Behold, his soul which is lifted up is not upright in him:
but the just shall live by his faith."
-Habakkuk 2:4 (KJV)

Using a Merriam-Webster dictionary resource, define the following terms:

Hypocrisy: (*noun*)

1._____
_____
2._____

Virtue: (*noun*)

1a._____
1b._____
3._____

Strife: (*noun*)

1a._____
1b._____
2._____
3.*archaic:*_____

Just: (*adjective*)

1a._____
1b._____
1c._____
2a.(1):_____
_____(2):_____
_____
2b._____

Creed: (*noun*)

1._____
2._____

Scripture Study – Habakkuk 2:1-4

1. According to verse 1, what is one of the jobs of the writer?

2. To Whom is the writer giving his attention?

3. What were the Lord's instructions in verse 2?

4. Why did the Lord command that the vision should be written?

5. According to verse 3, when is a vision from the Lord for?

6. What was the writer commanded to do even if the vision from the Lord did not come right away?

7. According to verse 4, what is not upright or righteous?

8. What shall the righteous, or just person live by?

9. What do you think this means?

10. Based on your studies this week, what questions do you have for your parents? Please write them on page 24.

Week 6

Scripture Memory Work: New Testament

"I tell you, this man went down to his house justified rather than the other: for every one that exalteth himself shall be abased; and he that humbleth himself shall be exalted."

-Luke 18:14 (KJV)

Using a Merriam-Webster dictionary resource, define the following terms:

Acquit: (*transitive verb*)
1a. *archaic:*_____
1b. *obsolete:*_____
2._____
3._____

Exalt: (*transitive verb*)
1._____
2._____
3. *obsolete:*_____
4._____
5._____

Abase: (*transitive verb*)
1._____
2._____

Justify: (*transitive verb*)
1a._____

Justify: (*intransitive verb*)
1a._____
1b._____

Scripture Study – Luke 18:9-14

Jesus is telling a story that is called a parable. Parables are earthly stories with heavenly meanings. Another term for a publican is a tax collector. Tax collectors were hated by most of the people, because they worked for the Roman government in Jesus' day. Pharisees were men who always went to church and were seen to do good things. As you study this parable, ask God to teach you about more about where your heart stands before Him.

1. According to verse 9, whom is Jesus teaching?

2. According to verse 10, how many men are in this story?

3. According to verses 11 & 12, who did the Pharisee exalt?

4. In verse 11, did the Pharisee speak well or poorly of the publican?

5. What sin filled the Pharisee's heart?

6. What was the publican's prayer?

7. What filled the publican's heart?

8. According to verse 14, whose heart and prayer pleased God?

9. Can you ever earn God's favor with your works?

10. Why should you seek to please God?

11. Based on your studies this week, what questions do you have for your parents? Please write them on page 24.

Questions for Parents:

Henry Francis Lyte (1793 – 1847)
Abide With Me

Abide with me; fast falls the eventide;
The darkness deepens; Lord with me abide.
When other helpers fail and comforts flee,
Help of the helpless, O abide with me.

Swift to its close ebbs out life's little day;
Earth's joys grow dim; its glories pass away;
Change and decay in all around I see;
O Thou who changest not, abide with me.

Not a brief glance I beg, a passing word,
But as Thou dwell'st with Thy disciples, Lord,
Familiar, condescending, patient, free.
Come not to sojourn, but abide with me.

Come not in terrors, as the King of kings,
But kind and good, with healing in Thy wings;
Tears for all woes, a heart for every plea.
Come, Friend of sinners, thus abide with me.

Thou on my head in early youth didst smile,
And though rebellious and perverse meanwhile,
Thou hast not left me, oft as I left Thee.
On to the close, O Lord, abide with me.

I need Thy presence every passing hour.
What but Thy grace can foil the tempter's power?
Who, like Thyself, my guide and stay can be?
Through cloud and sunshine, Lord, abide with me.

I fear no foe, with Thee at hand to bless;
Ills have no weight, and tears no bitterness.
Where is death's sting? Where, grave, thy victory?
I triumph still, if Thou abide with me.

Hold Thou Thy cross before my closing eyes;
Shine through the gloom and point me to the skies.
Heaven's morning breaks, and earth's vain shadows fl
In life, in death, O Lord, abide with me.

Abide With Me

Henry Francis Lyte (1793-1847)

"It is better to wear out than to rust out."

Do you know someone who seems to be sick all the time? Perhaps a good friend, or a well-loved family member, or maybe you yourself deal with sickness quite a bit. Yet even in sickness or frailty Jesus is there. He never leaves us. When our bodies have to fight to feel better, our Great Physician is by our side for the length of the battle.

Henry Francis Lyte was such a man. For all of his life, Henry dealt with health issues and had what others would call a "frail" life. In 1824, Henry would be called to the Devonshire area of England to pastor a church. He would share the love of Jesus with that area for more than twenty-four years, creating Sunday Schools for children, families and fishermen. He even started an annual outreach for 800-1,000 children that paired a gospel message with outdoor recreation! Can you just imagine? In Henry's day, there were no microphones or sound systems to help carry his voice when he would preach and teach. Yet in every service of worship to our great King, Henry would be completely dependent upon the strength that God would give him. God loved Henry. God strengthened him to do the work to which he was called.

If you are God's child, your Father loves you as well, and has work for you to do. The Apostle Paul called himself a "co-laborer" or a "co-worker" of Jesus. What a wonderful opportunity to work with Jesus, sharing His life and love! Even if we deal with frequent sickness, even if our bodies aren't always strong, God will give us just what we need to love Him, and others with our lives.

Toward the end of his life Henry was so sick that his friends and family urged him to rest, but Henry wanted to preach one last sermon. "It is better to wear out," he said playfully, "than to rust out." Everyone in the congregation listened attentively to every word of Henry's sermon on Communion with Jesus. That afternoon he handed a piece of paper to a dear relative. The top of the page held a Bible verse: Luke 24:29 – "Abide with us, for it is toward evening and the day is far spent." Following the Scripture there was a poem. The poem, of course, was "Abide with Me". Jesus would call Henry home to heaven just a few weeks later. His last words were heard to be "Joy! Peace!"

Even when you are weak, even when you are sick, Jesus is with you. Not only is He with you, His commands for you are the same. The next time He leads you through illness, think about Henry Francis Lyte. Examine your heart to see if Jesus' Spirit would lead you to be used greatly for God's glory, even in the midst of physical weakness. It really is better to wear out for God's Kingdom than to rust out in our own self-pity!

Week 7

Scripture Memory Work: Old Testament

"Be strong and of a good courage, fear not, nor be afraid of them: for the Lord thy God, he it is that doth go with thee; he will not fail thee, nor forsake thee."

-Deuteronomy 31:6 (KJV)

Using a Merriam-Webster dictionary resource, define the following terms:

Abide: (*intransitive verb*)
1._____
2._____

Ebb: (*Noun*)
1._____
2._____

Condescend: (*intransitive verb*)
1a._____
1b._____
2._____

Sojourn: (*Noun*)
1._____

Rebel: (*noun*)
1._____

Perverse: (*adjective*)
1a._____
1b._____
1c._____
_____
2a._____
2b._____

Scripture Study – Deuteronomy 31:1-6

1. Who is speaking in these verses?

2. How old is the speaker?

3. To whom is he speaking?

4. What was the promise to Israel from the Lord?

5. According to verse 6, from where does your strength and courage come?

6. According to verse 6, what is one of the greatest enemies to obeying God?

7. According to verse 6, does God ever leave His children?

8. Which one of these aspects of God's character does this describe? (Circle one)

    Omniscience   Omnipotence   Omnipresence

9. Are you strong and courageous all the time?

10. What do you think it means to be "frail"?

11. Are you independent of God, or dependent upon Him?

12. Based on your studies this week, what questions do you have for your parents? Please write them on page 32.

Week 8

Scripture Memory Work: New Testament

"And Jesus came and spake unto them, saying, 'All power is given unto me in heaven and in earth. Go ye therefore, and teach all nations, baptizing them in the name of the Father, and of the Son, and of the Holy Ghost: Teaching them to observe all things whatsoever I have commanded you: and, lo, I am with you always, even unto the end of the world. Amen.'"
-Matthew 28:18-20 (KJV)

Using a Merriam-Webster dictionary resource, define the following terms:

Foil: (*transitive verb*)
2a._____
2b._____

Triumph: (*noun*)
1._____
_____
_____
2._____
3a._____
3b._____

Gloom: (*noun*)
1a._____
1b._____
2a._____(b.)_____

Vain: (*adjective*)
1._____
2._____
3.*archaic:*_____
4._____
_____

Flee: (*verb*)
1a._____
1b._____

Scripture Study: Matthew 28: 16-20

1. Where did the disciples gather in this passage?

2. What were the two responses of the disciples to seeing Jesus after He rose again from the dead?

3. What does "authority" mean?

4. Why was Jesus given all authority in heaven and on earth?

5. What is Jesus commanding of his disciples (and us) in this passage?

6. What is a disciple?

7. What does it mean to "make disciples"?

8. What is the meaning of the following phrase : "to observe all that I have commanded you"? (verse 20)   Please circle one

    A. To watch commandments with your eyes

    B. To make a note of the commandments as only noble teachings

    C. To love Jesus' words so much, that His words change you in some way every day.

9. According to verse 20, will Jesus ever leave His people?

10. What is meant by "the end of the age"?

11. Based on your studies this week, what questions do you have for your parents? Please write them on page 32.

Questions for Parents:

William Walker

Come Ye Sinners, Poor and Needy (Music)

Come, ye sinners, poor and needy,
Weak and wounded, sick and sore;
Jesus ready stands to save you,
Full of pity, love and power.

Refrain
I will arise and go to Jesus,
He will embrace me in His arms;
In the arms of my dear Savior,
O there are ten thousand charms.

Come, ye thirsty, come, and welcome,
God's free bounty glorify;
True belief and true repentance,
Every grace that brings you nigh.

Come, ye weary, heavy laden,
Lost and ruined by the fall;
If you tarry till you're better,
You will never come at all.

View Him prostrate in the garden;
On the ground your Maker lies.
On the bloody tree behold Him;
Sinner, will this not suffice?

Lo! th'incarnate God ascended,
Pleads the merit of His blood:
Venture on Him, venture wholly,
Let no other trust intrude.

Let not conscience make you linger,
Not of fitness fondly dream;
All the fitness He requireth
Is to feel your need of Him.

Come Ye Sinners, Poor and Needy

Joseph Hart (1712 – 1768)

"In the arms of my dear Savior, oh there are ten thousand charms!"

Have you ever wondered what the gospel truly is? It is likely the word "gospel" is used at many of your church gatherings. Perhaps you have heard your parents or your pastor speak of the gospel. Perhaps you already know that it means "good news". But what is it really? What does it mean for your heart, your mind, your life and your future? Is the gospel just something to be believed with your mind, or is it something more?

Joseph Hart struggled with these questions for many, many years. He grew up with parents who loved Jesus very much. They taught him from the Bible, just like many of you! Many times, however, he would still have questions. As he grew, so did the questions in his mind. There was even a point in Joseph's life where he would live very selfishly and hurt others with his choices. Perhaps you have had times in your life like that. We can be deceived into thinking that the way we live has no effect on others. But God made us all to be connected in some way to other people, whether they are family or friends that He has given.

Joseph claimed to believe the gospel, but his heart was far from God. The good news of the gospel is only good to people who have been captured by Jesus' love. You see, when God saves a person, they are "born again." Nothing about them is the same as when it was without Jesus! If the Spirit of God gives you new birth, your heart is fixed on your Heavenly Father. Your mind seeks to know Him for Who He is, and not Who you would make Him to be. Your affections change, your attitudes change, your hope is only in Jesus.

When Joseph's heart was changed, he began to realize that a relationship with God was more than getting the answers right on a test. The Spirit of God taught Joseph that there was never a moment to be lived outside of Jesus' love. Instead of living for himself, Joseph began to live a life of love for Jesus. Everything he did, everything he said was a response of Jesus' love for him. Joseph was an entirely different person. Yes, the gospel is found in the Bible's stories of Jesus' life, death, resurrection, ascension and reign. Yes, the gospel is the truth that God saves people. But Joseph was not content until God captured him with the beauty and love of Jesus. Only then did the gospel become the power of salvation for him.

Perhaps there are questions in your heart about the gospel, and what it means to truly be saved by Jesus. I assure you that there are no greater questions in the world! As you sing *Come Ye Sinners, Poor and Needy* in the coming weeks, do not be afraid of any questions that may come. No one can go to Jesus for you. You must go to Him yourself. Meet with Him today, and see for yourself if He truly does have "ten thousand charms"!

Week 9

Scripture Memory Work: Old Testament

"The sacrifices of God are a broken spirit: a broken and a contrite heart, O God, thou wilt not despise."

-Psalm 51:17 (KJV)

Using a Merriam-Webster dictionary resource, define the following terms:

Pity: (*noun*)

1a._____

1b._____

2._____

Embrace: (*transitive verb*)

1a._____

1b._____

2._____

3a._____

3b._____

Bounty: (*noun*)

1._____

2._____

3._____

4._____

Venture: (*transitive verb*)

1._____

2._____

3._____

Scripture Study – Psalm 51:1-12

King David wrote this psalm to ask God to forgive him for the sins that he committed. As you study this week, grow in the knowledge that God does truly forgive you as you turn from your sin.

1. What is David asking for in verse 1?

2. According to the requests in verse 2, what do you think sin does to a person?

3. According to verse 3, what is important for a person who is repenting to do?

4. According to verse 4, Who is the first Person that sin offends?

5. According to verse 5, how long have we been sinful?

6. According to verse 6, what does God desire?

7. According to verse 8, what does the guilt of sin sometimes feel like?

8. According to verse 10, Who has the power to create a clean heart?

9. According to verse 12, what does forgiveness from God restore?

10. Based on your studies this week, what questions do you have for your parents? Please write them on page 40.

Week 10

Scripture Memory Work: New Testament

"If we confess our sins, he is faithful and just to forgive us our sins, and to cleanse us from all unrighteousness."

-1 John 1:9 (KJV)

Using a Merriam-Webster dictionary resource, define the following terms:

Repent: (*intransitive verb*)
1._____
_____
2a._____
2b._____

Incarnate: (*adjective*)
1a._____
_____
1b._____
_____

Weary: (*adjective*)
1._____
_____
2._____
_____
3._____
_____

Suffice: (*verb*)
Intransitive
1._____
_____
_____
2._____
_____

Transitive
1._____

Scripture Study – 1 John 1:3-10

1. According to verse 3, what does John declare?

2. According to verses 3 & 4, why does John declare it?

3. According to verse 5, what is the message that John declares?

4. According to verse 6, can we walk in darkness and say we are God's children?

5. According to verse 7, where must we walk if we are God's children?

6. What do you think it means to "walk in the light"?

7. According to verse 8, what do we do if we think we have no sin?

8. According to verse 9, what will happen if we confess our sins to God?

9. According to verse 10, what happens if we try to hide or deny our sins?

10. Based on your studies this week, what questions do you have for your parents? Please write them on page 40.

Questions for Parents:

George Croly (1780 – 1860)
Spirit of God, Descend Upon My Heart

Spirit of God, descend upon my heart;
Wean it from earth; through all its pulses move;
Stoop to my weakness, mighty as Thou art;
And make me love Thee as I ought to love.

I ask no dream, no prophet ecstasies,
No sudden rending of the veil of clay,
No angel visitant, no opening skies;
But take the dimness of my soul away.

Teach me to feel that Thou art always nigh;
Teach me the struggles of the soul to bear.
To check the rising doubt, the rebel sigh,
Teach me the patience of unanswered prayer.

Hast Thou not bid me love Thee, God and King?
All, all Thine own, soul, heart and strength and mind.
I see Thy cross; there teach my heart to cling:
O let me seek Thee, and O let me find!

Teach me to love Thee as Thine angels love,
One holy passion filling all my frame;
The kindling of the heaven descended Dove,
My heart an altar, and Thy love the flame.

Spirit of God, Descend Upon My Heart
George Croly (1780-1860)
"One holy passion filling all my frame."

Have you ever undertaken a task so difficult that its accomplishment seems impossible? Perhaps it is a project given to you for school. Perhaps it is a really big chore around your house. Perhaps it is a task that everyone you know has forsaken. Yet even when things seem hopeless or impossible, Jesus is there! He always has a plan. He is Wisdom itself. He knows just how to get things done, and He is your greatest source of help.

George Croly was no stranger to difficult tasks. Born and raised in Dublin, Ireland, George went to Trinity College. He studied to be a minister of the gospel of Jesus and would later move to London, England. He would look for difficult projects to undertake. Soon after settling in London, George would re-open St. Stephen's Church in a poor part of the city. St. Stephen's had been closed and abandoned for over a century! It was very obvious that no one thought a church could grow in that poor neighborhood. Did that stop George? Of course not! He believed that Jesus would help him and give him wisdom.

Sometimes you must look beyond the difficulties that you see. Sometimes you must teach your ears to hear Jesus' words that "with God, all things are possible!" (Matt. 19:26) Surely there is great evidence in the Bible for this! You must remember that whatever you do, it is all for the glory of God (1 Corinthians 10:31). So, even in your trying, whether you succeed or fail in the eyes of men, your heart before God is full of love. You must be content in whatever labors the Lord gives to you, knowing that He is pleased with your obedience.

There were many of George's friends who thought he was crazy to re-open St. Stephen's Church. Yet St. Stephen's is still growing and active today because he did! They have sent out dozens of missionaries with the gospel of Jesus to places all over the world. God wanted that poor community in London to know His love and care. He gave George grace and strength to do what other people called impossible. George would know very well the struggles of his soul, but he would give those struggles to Jesus.

Perhaps God will ask you to do something very difficult. What a blessing that would be! God dreams very big dreams, and plans very big plans. If He asks you to do something difficult, remember George Croly. Jesus gave George His dream for the poor people of London, and the grace and courage to obey. Jesus will do no less for you! With God, there is no such thing as failure.

Week 11

Scripture Memory Work: Old Testament

"Then Samuel took the horn of oil, and anointed him in the midst of his brethren: and the Spirit of the Lord came upon David from that day forward. So Samuel rose up, and went to Ramah."

-I Samuel 16:13 (KJV)

Using a Merriam-Webster dictionary resource, define the following terms:

Descend: (*intransitive verb*)

1._____

2._____

3a._____

3b._____

3c._____

4._____

Anoint: (*transitive verb*)

1._____

2a._____

2b._____

Ruddy: (*adjective*)

1._____

2._____

Countenance: (*noun*)

1.*obsolete:*_____

2a._____

2b._____

2c._____

4._____

Scripture Study – 1 Samuel 16:1-13

In this passage, God sends Samuel the prophet on a top-secret mission to anoint David as the new king in Israel. Saul, the old king, was still alive but he did not honor God with his heart.

1. In verse 1, to whom was God sending Samuel?

2. Where was God sending Samuel?

3. According to verse 2, of who was Samuel afraid?

4. What was God's plan in verse 2 & 3?

5. When all the people at Jesse's house assembled for the sacrifice, who was the first son to stand before Samuel?

6. Did God choose him?

7. According to verse 7, at what was Samuel looking?

8. Does the Lord see things like we do?

9. What does the Lord look upon?

10. According to verse 10, how many sons did Jesse set before Samuel and God?

11. Were there any more sons? (verse 11)

12. Where was the youngest son?

13. Based on your studies this week, what questions do you have for your parents? Please write them on page 48.

Week 12

Scripture Memory Work: New Testament

"For if ye live after the flesh, ye shall die: but if ye through the Spirit do mortify the deeds of the body, ye shall live. For as many as are led by the Spirit of God, they are the sons of God."

-Romans 8:13-14 (KJV)

Using a Merriam-Webster dictionary resource, define the following terms:

Rend: (*intransitive verb*)
1._____
2._____

Kindling: (*noun*)
1._____

Witness: (*transitive verb*)
1._____
2._____
3._____

Heir: (*noun*)
1._____
_____
2._____
_____
3._____
_____

Adopt: (*transitive verb*)
1._____
_____
2._____
3._____
_____

Scripture Study – Romans 8:13-18

1. Verse 13 speaks of "the deeds of the body". The Apostle Paul uses these words to describe our sin. What are God's children to do through the power of the Spirit?

2. What does it mean to "mortify"?

3. According to verse 14, Who leads the children of God?

4. According to verse 15, what spirit have God's children **NOT** received?

5. What is the Spirit that God's children received?

6. According to verse 16, Who bears witness whether or not we are God's child?

7. According to verse 17, God's children are heirs. What will God's children inherit?

8. In verse 17, what must God's children endure?

9. According to verse 18, will the sufferings that God's children endure compare with the glory they will see?

10. Based on your studies this week, what questions do you have for your parents? Please write them on page 48.

Questions for Parents:

Bernard of Clairvaux (1090 – 1153)
Jesus, the Very Thought of Thee

Jesus, the very thought of Thee
With sweetness fills the breast;
But sweeter far Thy face to see,
And in Thy presence rest.

Nor voice can sing, nor heart can frame,
Nor can the memory find
A sweeter sound than Thy blest Name,
O Savior of mankind!

O hope of every contrite heart,
O joy of all the meek,
To those who fall, how kind Thou art!
How good to those who seek!

But what to those who find? Ah, this
Nor tongue nor pen can show;
The love of Jesus, what it is,
None but His loved ones know.

Jesus, our only joy be Thou,
As Thou our prize will be;
Jesus be Thou our glory now,
And through eternity.

O Jesus, King most wonderful
Thou Conqueror renowned,
Thou sweetness most ineffable
In Whom all joys are found!

O Jesus, light of all below,
Thou fount of living fire,
Surpassing all the joys we know,
And all we can desire.

Jesus, the Very Thought of Thee

Bernard of Clairvaux (1090 – 1153)

"What we love we shall grow to resemble."

Is there someone in your life that you consider a hero? Perhaps someone very special whom you admire? You find yourself watching and waiting just to spend time with them again! You love to hear their words. You enjoy the attention and affection they give to you. You find a desire within your heart to be just like them. God gives us many gifts in people that we may love and follow. The greatest gift God gave us was His Son, Jesus. Jesus is the greatest hero we could ever hope to know!

Bernard of Clairvaux's life was full of heroes. He grew up in a French nobleman's home almost a thousand years ago. Being nobility, Bernard enjoyed many luxuries for which most French people could only hope. He had an excellent education from parents who loved him. When he was only a young man Bernard encountered a great sadness upon the death of his mother. Instead of being angry and running away from God, Bernard ran to his greatest hero, Jesus. Bernard sought to join the church as a monk. Monks were men who would live solitary lives devoted to God. Bernard would join other monks whose focus was working in nature. He would farm crops, keep bees, and even brew ales!

Sometimes our lives are not always happy. Sometimes our lives are marked with sadness or tragedy. We need to know that Jesus' arms are always open. We can run to Him in joy and sorrow. He wants to hear us talk to Him. He wants us to listen to Him as well.

As Bernard grew up, he showed others that he was a leader by serving them and doing all he was asked. The church made him an Abbot, which means he was in charge of taking care of the other monks. Bernard named the valley of his Abbey "Claire Vallee", or "Clear Valley". The place, which is in the northeast part of France, became known as "Clairvaux". Bernard became a very influential man both in the church and in politics as he grew older. He even had to travel all over Europe to settle disputes. Bernard would write many hymns that would help people see Jesus' beauty and power and love. *Jesus, the Very Thought of Thee* has fifteen verses that explore high thoughts of Jesus, and just how good He is to those who find Him.

Who are your heroes? Do you think of Jesus as one? Bernard once said, "What we love, we shall grow to resemble." Our sin, at its root, is our failure to love Jesus as we should love Him. But He has grace and patience for His children who repent! What a great hero He is! He wants our heart. As He captures our affections, He makes us to resemble Him more and more. As we look more like Him, He is glorified, our lives are made rich, and other people are blessed. Other heroes will, at some point, let you down. Jesus is a hero unlike any other.

Week 13

Scripture Memory Work: Old Testament

"Seek the Lord, and his strength: seek his face evermore."

-Psalm 105:4 (KJV)

Using a Merriam-Webster dictionary resource, define the following terms:

Frame: (*transitive verb*)

1._____

_____

2a._____

2b._____

2c._____

2d._____

Contrite: (*adjective*)

1._____

_____

Meek: (*adjective*)

1._____

_____

2._____

3._____

Renown: (*noun*)

1._____

_____

2.*obsolete:*_____

Ineffable: (*adjective*)

1a._____

1b._____

2._____

Scripture Study – Psalm 105:1-8

1. What are the three things God's people are to do in verse 1?

2. According to verse 3, what are we to glory in?

3. What is our heart to do as we seek the Lord? (verse 3)

4. According to verse 4, when are we to seek the Lord and His strength?

5. Verse 5 tells us to remember God's marvelous works. Please write some of His works that you remember below:

6. Verse 7 states that God's "judgments are in all the earth." This speaks of His ruling and reigning. Name some examples of God reigning in the earth:

7. What does verse 8 mean when it speaks of God remembering His covenant?

8. Based on your studies this week, what questions do you have for your parents? Please write them on page 56.

Week 14

Scripture Memory Work: New Testament

"And to know the love of Christ, which passeth knowledge, that ye might be filled with all the fullness of God."
-Ephesians 3:19 (KJV)

Using a Merriam-Webster dictionary resource, define the following terms:

Cause: (*noun*)
1a._____
1b._____
1c._____
_____
1d._____

Comprehend: (*transitive verb*)
1._____
_____
2._____
_____
3._____
_____

Grant: (*transitive verb*)
1a._____
_____
1b._____
_____
2._____
3a._____
3b._____

Exceed: (*transitive verb*)
1._____
2._____
3._____

Scripture Study – Ephesians 3:14-21

The Apostle Paul wrote this letter to a church in Asia Minor in the city of Ephesus. Our passage this week is a prayer from his heart to the believers in the church.

1. In verses 14 & 15, of Whom is the whole family in heaven and earth named?

2. Of what family is Paul speaking in verse 15?

3. In verse 16, Paul describes God's glory as a treasure chest full of riches. What does Paul ask God to do for the believers in verse 16?

4. What is Paul's prayer request in verse 17?

5. According to verse 17, in what are we to be rooted and grounded?

6. What four measurements does Paul give in verse 18?

7. A paradox is a statement that seems to contradict itself, yet is true. What paradox is found in verse 19?

8. According to verse 20, what is God able to do?

9. According to verse 21, how long should God receive glory?

10. Based on your studies this week, what questions do you have for your parents? Please write them on page 56.

Questions for Parents:

Edward Perronet (1726 – 1792)
All Hail the Power of Jesus' Name

All hail the power of Jesus' name!
Let angels prostrate fall;
Bring forth the royal diadem,
And crown Him Lord of all.
Bring forth the royal diadem,
And crown Him Lord of all.

Ye chosen seed of Israel's race,
Ye ransomed from the fall,
Hail Him who saves you by his grace,
And crown Him Lord of all.
Hail Him who saves you by his grace,
And crown Him Lord of all.

Sinners, whose love can ne'er forget
The wormwood and the gall,
Go spread your trophies at His feet,
And crown Him Lord of all.
Go spread your trophies at His feet,
And crown Him Lord of all.

Let every kindred, every tribe
On this terrestrial ball,
To Him all majesty ascribe,
And crown Him Lord of all.
To Him all majesty ascribe,
And crown Him Lord of all.

Crown him, ye martyrs of your God,
Who from His altar call;
Extol the Stem of Jesse's Rod,
And crown Him Lord of all.
Extol the Stem of Jesse's Rod,
And crown Him Lord of all.

O that with yonder sacred throng
We at His feet may fall!
To join the everlasting song,
And crown Him Lord of all.
To join the everlasting song,
And crown Him Lord of all.

All Hail the Power of Jesus' Name

Edward Perronet (1726 – 1792)

"Glory to God in His all-sufficiency!"

Are you a shy person by nature? Perhaps you do not have any problem expressing yourself to others. Then again, perhaps you do! Is it difficult trying to explain how you are feeling or what you are thinking? Does the thought of standing before a crowd and speaking make you nervous? You need to know that even though you are shy, Jesus is with you!

Edward Perronet was a shy person at times. He grew up in the Church of England. His grandfather and father were ministers. Edward knew many truths that the Bible taught him of Jesus. He would become fast friends with the Wesley brothers, John and Charles. There were many occasions when John would ask Edward to preach, but Edward would always say "no". He did not think he could preach as well as John Wesley. Edward was a skilled preacher but was shy when John was present. Perhaps you can relate to Edward in some way! Perhaps you, like him, find it easier to express yourself in writing. Oh, how Edward would write! He loved crafting thoughts and milling through sentences. God gives each of us a beautifully unique way of finding our voice to the world.

All Hail the Power of Jesus' Name is Edward's most famous hymn. Many people call it "Christianity's Anthem". In it, Edward paints a marvelous picture of the entire universe in constant worship of Jesus. He speaks of angels with instruments falling down before the Master Conductor. Stars and planets lend their voice to the never-ending song! There is a verse for all who trusted Jesus, even to their death. Every tribe and tongue and nation is called upon to cast all trophies at Jesus' feet. Edward even beckons to us to remember how much Jesus loves us. We must never forget the awful cross where Jesus purchased salvation for those the Father has given Him.

When you think of King Jesus, what does your mind see? Is He strong? Is He courageous? Is He kind? It is important to always think of Jesus rightly! Our thoughts about Him must always be carried by the words of the Bible. Sometimes, our thoughts of Jesus may inspire awe and fear. Some thoughts are just too much for us. Everyone who truly knows God experiences this. You are in good company!

C. S. Lewis, author of *The Chronicles of Narnia*, explains those feelings well. The hero of his *Chronicles* is a mighty lion named Aslan, who lays down his life for a traitor. After he dies, Aslan rises again from the dead! Does that sound like anyone else you know? Aslan, as Lewis describes him, is "not a tame lion, but he is good". The same can be said for Jesus. We cannot tame Him. We cannot control Him. But He is good! He is the best King we could ever hope to have! He is trustworthy and true. In the following weeks, ask Jesus to help you see Him for Who He really is.

Week 15

Scripture Memory Work: Old Testament

"Lift up your heads, O ye gates; and be ye lift up, ye everlasting doors; and the King of glory shall come in. Who is this King of glory? The Lord strong and mighty, the Lord mighty in battle."

-Psalm 24:7-8 (KJV)

Using a Merriam-Webster dictionary resource, define the following terms:

Diadem: (*noun*)

1._____

2._____

Ransom: (*transitive verb*)

1._____

_____

2._____

_____

Hail: (*transitive verb*)

1a._____

1b._____

2._____

Kindred: (*noun*)

1a._____

1b._____

2._____

Ascribe: (*transitive verb*)

1._____

_____

Scripture Study -- Psalm 24:1-10

1. According to verse 1, to Whom does the earth belong?

2. According to verse 4, who shall stand in God's presence?

3. What shall the upright in heart receive from God? (verse 5)

4. To whom is the psalmist calling attention in verse 7?

5. What are the everlasting doors spoken of in verse 7?

6. How is the King of Glory described in verse 8?

7. If Jesus is the King of Glory, where do you think He fought His greatest battle?

8. What enemies did He defeat?

9. Based on your studies this week, what questions do you have for your parents? Please write them on page 64.

Week 16

Scripture Memory Work: New Testament

"That at the name of Jesus every knee should bow, of things in heaven, and things in earth, and things under the earth; And that every tongue should confess that Jesus Christ is Lord, to the glory of God the Father."
-Philippians 2:10-11 (KJV)

Using a Merriam-Webster dictionary resource, define the following terms:

Reputation: (*noun*)

1a._____

1b._____

2._____

Humble: (*adjective*)

1._____

2._____

3a._____

3b._____

Prostrate: (*adjective*)

1._____

2._____

3._____

Terrestrial: (*adjective*)

1a._____

1b._____

Scripture Study -- Philippians 2:5-13

1. The Apostle Paul describes the mind of Jesus in verses 6-8. As you read these verses, what words would you use?

2. According to verse 5, who else is to have these attitudes?

3. According to verse 9, what was Jesus' reward for His obedience?

4. According to verse 10, what will every knee do?

5. What will every tongue do?

6. According to verse 11, why will every knee and tongue do this?

7. In verse 12, Paul tells us that our obedience should not be limited to the times that we are with our parents or authority figures, but in their absence as well. Who is always with us, even when our parents are not?

8. According to verse 13, what work does God the Father do in the hearts of His children?

9. Based on your studies this week, what questions do you have for your parents? Please write them on page 64.

Questions for Parents:

Samuel J. Stone (1839 – 1900)
The Church's One Foundation

The Church's one foundation
Is Jesus Christ her Lord,
She is His new creation
By water and the Word.
From heaven He came and sought her
To be His holy bride;
With His own blood He bought her
And for her life He died.

She is from every nation,
Yet one o'er all the earth;
Her charter of salvation,
One Lord, one faith, one birth;
One holy Name she blesses,
Partakes one holy food,
And to one hope she presses,
With every grace endued.

The Church shall never perish!
Her dear Lord to defend,
To guide, sustain, and cherish,
Is with her to the end:
Though there be those who hate her,
And false sons in her pale,
Against both foe or traitor
She ever shall prevail.

Though with a scornful wonder
Men see her sore oppressed,
By schisms rent asunder,
By heresies distressed:
Yet saints their watch are keeping,
Their cry goes up, "How long?"
And soon the night of weeping
Shall be the morn of song!

'Mid toil and tribulation,
And tumult of her war,
She waits the consummation
Of peace forevermore;
Till, with the vision glorious,
Her longing eyes are blest,
And the great Church victorious
Shall be the Church at rest.

Yet she on earth hath union
With God the Three in One,
And mystic sweet communion
With those whose rest is won,
With all her sons and daughters
Who, by the Master's hand
Led through the deathly waters,
Repose in Eden land.

The Church's One Foundation
Samuel J. Stone (1839-1900)
"Soon the night of weeping shall be the morn of song."

Is it sometimes difficult for you to do your studies? There are many things that vie for our attention. We enjoy games, entertainment and recreation. The hard things, the parts of our lives that demand focus, are oftentimes the things that we tend to "forget". Yet even in our laziness, Jesus is there. He gives us diligence if we ask it of Him. He gives us able and ready teachers. He equips those teachers to form study tools to help us when it feels like we want to quit.

One such teacher Jesus gave His church was Samuel J. Stone. Samuel attended some of the very best schools and universities in England. In the 1800's, many of the poor people of England did not know how to read and write. Samuel would spend much of his time reaching out to the poor. So much time, in fact, he became known as "the poor man's pastor". Samuel would open his church doors every morning at 6:30 so that people on their way to work, frequently poor young girls, could have a brief service and prayer, then have time to rest, to read or to sew. He built numerous churches; his belief was that poor people deserved beautiful churches in which to worship. Most of the hymns that Samuel wrote were based on stories that Jesus told to poor people in His time. These stories are called parables. God used Samuel's songs to teach the truth of the Bible to people who couldn't read! Isn't that wonderful? God used Samuel to show that it does not matter how much money you have, that Jesus died for poor people as well as the rich.

There are many tools that God's children have been given in His church. One of these tools is called a creed. Simply put, a creed is a list of truths based on the Bible that Christians use to remind themselves of the holiness of God and His great work of redemption. Very often, because of sin and the hardness of our hearts, creeds can become boring, lifeless things. So, because of this, Samuel would write hymns to express the heart of the creeds. "The Church's One Foundation" is such a hymn. It finds itself in part of The Apostle's Creed, which you may have spoken before in one of your gatherings with God's people.

If you are God's child, the most important thing you can ever do with your whole life is to know your heavenly Father. There is no greater knowledge than the knowledge of the Living God Who passionately pursues His children. We are commanded to worship God with all of our minds. As we do, we should pray that our Father would use our minds for His glory. We should ask Him to use our knowledge of Him to set our hearts on fire with love for Him. The next time you are discouraged in your studies, think of Samuel. Ask God to give you tools to grow your mind for His glory and your good!

Week 17

Scripture Memory Work: Old Testament

"My soul, wait thou only upon God; for my expectation is from him. He only is my rock and my salvation: he is my defense; I shall not be moved. In God is my salvation and my glory: the rock of my strength, and my refuge, is in God."
-Psalm 62:5-7 (KJV)

Using a Merriam-Webster dictionary resource, define the following terms:

Foundation: (*noun*)

1._____
2._____

Charter: (*noun*)

1._____
2a._____

2b._____

Partake: (*intransitive verb*)

1._____
2._____
3._____

For "Endue", use "Endow" (*transitive verb*)

1._____

2._____
3._____

Perish: (*intransitive verb*)

1._____

Scripture Study -- Psalm 62: 5-12

1. To whom is the writer speaking?

2. About Whom is the writer speaking?

3. How is God like a rock or a fortress?

4. What is meant by the words "pour out your heart before God"?

5. According to verse 8, when should people put their trust in God?

6. Verse 9 speaks of balances or scales that would be used to weigh something. Does money cause God to think more highly of you? Explain your answer.

7. Of what does verse 10 warn us?

8. In verse 12, what is meant by "steadfast love"?

9. What is meant by "For you will render to a man according to his work"?

10. Based on your studies this week, what questions do you have for your parents? Please write them on page 72.

Week 18

Scripture Memory Work: New Testament

"Now therefore ye are no more strangers and foreigners, but fellow citizens with the saints, and of the household of God; And are built upon the foundation of the apostles and prophets, Jesus Christ himself being the chief corner stone; In whom all the building fitly framed together groweth unto an holy temple in the Lord."
-Ephesians 2:19-21 (KJV)

Using a Merriam-Webster dictionary resource, define the following terms:

Schism: (*noun*)

1._____
2a._____
_____
2b._____

Asunder: (*adverb* or *adjective*)

1._____
2._____

Toil: (*noun*)

1a._____
1b._____
2._____

Tribulation: (*noun*)

1._____
_____

Communion: (*noun*)

1._____
2a._____
_____
_____
3._____
4._____

Scripture Study -- Ephesians 2:13-22

1. According to verse 19, what was once our relationship to God?

2. According to verse 13, if we are in Jesus, are we strangers to God or near to Him?

3. What is Jesus called in verse 14?

4. Verse 16 speaks of Jesus "reconciling" us to God. What does it mean to "be reconciled" to God?

5. According to verse 16, what did God use to reconcile His children to Himself?

6. According to verse 18, how do God's children have access to Him?

7. What is the foundation of the apostles and prophets mentioned in verse 20?

8. Who is the Cornerstone mentioned in verse 20?

9. What is a Cornerstone?

10. According to verse 22, how are God's children built together?

11. Based on your studies this week, what questions do you have for your parents? Please write them on page 72.

Questions for Parents:

William Williams (1717 – 1791)
Guide Me O Thou Great Jehovah

Guide me, O Thou great Jehovah,
Pilgrim through this barren land.
I am weak, but Thou art mighty;
Hold me with Thy powerful hand.
Bread of Heaven, Bread of Heaven,
Feed me till I want no more;
Feed me till I want no more.

Open now the crystal fountain,
Whence the healing stream doth flow;
Let the fire and cloudy pillar
Lead me all my journey through.
Strong Deliverer, strong Deliverer,
Be Thou still my Strength and Shield;
Be Thou still my Strength and Shield.

Lord, I trust Thy mighty power,
Wondrous are Thy works of old;
Thou deliver'st Thine from thralldom,
Who for naught themselves had sold:
Thou didst conquer, Thou didst conquer,
Sin, and Satan and the grave,
Sin, and Satan and the grave.

When I tread the verge of Jordan,
Bid my anxious fears subside;
Death of deaths, and hell's destruction,
Land me safe on Canaan's side.
Songs of praises, songs of praises,
I will ever give to Thee;
I will ever give to Thee.

Musing on my habitation,
Musing on my heav'nly home,
Fills my soul with holy longings:
Come, my Jesus, quickly come;
Vanity is all I see;
Lord, I long to be with Thee!
Lord, I long to be with Thee!

Guide Me O Thou Great Jehovah

William Williams (1717 – 1791)

"Thou didst conquer sin and Satan and the grave!"

Have you ever been interrupted? You may be right in the middle of a thought or a sentence when all of a sudden an ambush is upon you! Interruptions are a big part of life, for better or worse. Whether they are from your little brother or sister, or from a parent calling to you, interruptions can be very frustrating! Now, think for a moment. Have you ever been interrupted by *God*? What do you think that may look or feel like?

William Williams was certainly interrupted by God. He was in medical school. He had strong desires to be a doctor and to help people. While that is a wonderful job to have, God had other ideas for William. Remember, God dreams big dreams! One Sunday William was taking a walk in the countryside of Wales. As he walked by a church William saw a young man standing on top of a tombstone preaching. A crowd was gathered around the young preacher. William stopped to listen. The preacher talked and sang about life with Jesus. William was wonderfully saved that day! He decided to leave medical school and enter the ministry. He would serve as a deacon in two area churches for several years. He soon became a very good friend to George Whitefield, who brought the gospel in power to America. It wasn't long before God ambushed William with another desire: to preach the gospel in all of Wales. For forty-three years William traveled all over his country on horseback. Many people estimate him to have ridden over 100,000 miles in all! His preaching style, coupled with his sweet singing voice, was used to glorify God and draw many people to Him. William's hymns were often inspired by the countryside as he traveled. He would use pictures of the grandeur of nature to communicate intimate truths about Jesus' love.

What dreams are you dreaming about your life? Perhaps you are a critical thinker. Perhaps you enjoy numbers and mathematics. There are those of us who love history and geography with a passion for world civilizations. Many of us love science - every form of it! Then there are, of course, the artists. Painters, dancers and musicians all have different methods to find inspiration! The passions and interests you have are from God. He meant for you to have them. So as you grow in them, keep your heart open to His interruptions. Remember William, and the life that God gave to him.

William wrote more than 900 hymns. His was a heart that overflowed with a love for Jesus. That is the most important part of life, after all. Every good gift and talent is from His hand. Every task that we undertake is to be to His glory. Remember that as you have many adventures, to leave room for His interruptions. Your life will be all the more rich if you do!

Week 19

Scripture Memory Work: Old Testament

"A man's heart deviseth his way: but the Lord directeth his steps."

-Proverbs 16:9 (KJV)

Using a Merriam-Webster dictionary resource, define the following terms:

Pilgrim: (*noun*)

1._____

2._____

3.*capitalized*:_____

Thrall: (*noun*)

1a._____

1b._____

2a._____

2b._____

Conquer: (*transitive verb*)

1._____

2._____

3._____

4._____

Subside: (*intransitive verb*)

1._____

2._____

3._____

4._____

Scripture Study – Proverbs 16:1-9

The book of Proverbs was written by King David's son, whose name is Solomon. It is a book of wisdom, and was given to us so that we may better know how we ought to live. The 16th chapter of Proverbs contrasts the difference between people's plans and those of the Lord.

1. In verse 2, how do people see their own choices?

2. Who knows their hearts and true intentions?

3. According to verse 3, how shall your thoughts be established?

4. According to verse 4, for what are the wicked made?

5. According to verse 5, what is offensive or an abomination to God?

6. According to verse 6, how is iniquity purged?

7. How do men depart from evil? (verse 6)

8. What is one of the benefits of pleasing the Lord found in verse 7?

9. According to verse 8, which is a better thing: to be rich or to please God?

10. According to verse 9, even if we make our plans, Who directs our steps?

11. Based on your studies this week, what questions do you have for your parents? Please write them on page 80.

Week 20

Scripture Memory Work: New Testament

"But seek ye first the kingdom of God, and his righteousness; and all these things shall be added unto you."

-Matthew 6:33 (KJV)

Using a Merriam-Webster dictionary resource, define the following terms:

Anxious: (*adjective*)

1._____

_____

_____

2._____

_____

3._____

Muse: (*intransitive verb*)

1._____

_____

_____

_____

2.*archaic*:_____

Righteous: (*adjective*)

1._____

_____

2a._____

2b._____

_____

Splendor: (*noun*)

1a._____

1b._____

2._____

Scripture Study – Matthew 6:25-34

In this passage, Jesus is preaching His sermon on the mount. This week, we will study what He says about being anxious. Jesus uses humor in this part of His sermon to point out how silly it is not to trust the Father with everything.

1. What does Jesus tell us not to worry about in verse 25?

2. What example does Jesus give in verse 26?

3. Do you ever see birds farming? How do they eat?

4. Read verse 27. Can you grow taller by just thinking that you can?

5. What example does Jesus give in verse 28?

6. Have you ever seen flowers shopping for clothes? Who clothes them?

7. According to verse 32, Who knows what our needs are?

8. According to verse 33, with what should God's children be concerned?

9. Based on your studies this week, what questions do you have for your parents? Please write them on page 80.

Questions for Parents:

Christina Rossetti (1830 – 1894)
None Other Lamb

None other Lamb, none other Name,
None other hope in Heav'n or earth or sea,
None other hiding place from guilt and shame,
None beside Thee!

My faith burns low, my hope burns low;
Only my heart's desire cries out in me
By the deep thunder of its want and woe,
Cries out to Thee.

Lord, Thou art Life, though I be dead;
Love's fire Thou art, however cold I be:
Nor Heav'n have I, nor place to lay my head,
Nor home, but Thee.

None Other Lamb

Christina Rossetti (1830 – 1894)

"My heart is like a singing bird."

Do you like adventures? Do you seem to find adventure wherever you may go? Perhaps your imagination is always taking you to faraway lands. Perhaps you enjoy being an explorer or a princess or a soldier. So often, we don't think about Jesus in the middle of our adventures. Yet He is there! The Bible says in the gospel of John that all things were made by Him. He is the original adventurer! All the colors and sights and sounds and smells that you enjoy were His idea.

Christina Rossetti had quite an adventurous life. She was the youngest of four children. Her father called Christina and her brother Dante Gabriel his "two storms." The other two children, Maria and William, he called his "two calms." What would your parents call you? Christina's family was a writing family. They had their schooling at home. Before she could even write, Christina would ask her mother to write down the stories that she told. As Christina grew, her family would begin to publish a newspaper at home. Her grandfather would even print her poems on his own printing press! She would often take walks to the London Zoo as well as the newly opened Regent's Park. Of all the places she would go, she loved her grandfather's house most of all. In a letter to a friend, she wrote, "If any one thing schooled me in the direction of poetry, it was perhaps the delightful idle liberty to prowl all alone about my grandfather's cottage-grounds some thirty miles from London."

Perhaps you have a favorite spot where you like to "prowl". Perhaps you like to have adventures and create stories with special loved ones. You can be sure that God is the most creative Person in the universe. The adventure of redemption that He has written is the most exciting adventure you could ever read. It is the story of a King Who died for His enemies. It is the story of a King Who came to life again to make those enemies His children. It is your story as well, if you are indeed His child!

When Christina got older, she would fight sickness, as we all do. After one such fight, she would write a work called *Annus Domini: A Prayer for Each Day of the Year*. This publication would have 366 devotional writings in poetry and prose in which Christina would paint beautiful word pictures to show the beauty of Jesus.

You can make up stories to glorify the greatest Hero that ever lived: the God-Man Jesus Christ. Many authors have written stories about Him as a lion, a warrior, a king, a shepherd, a priest, a spaceman or even a bus driver! When Jesus would tell stories about Himself, He would call Himself a farmer, a vineyard owner, and a doctor. In the coming weeks, try to create adventures that glorify Jesus as the sure, strong and coming King.

Week 21

Scripture Memory Work: Old Testament

"The Lord thy God in the midst of thee is mighty; he will save, he will rejoice over thee with joy; he will rest in his love, he will joy over thee with singing."

-Zephaniah 3:17 (KJV)

Using a Merriam-Webster dictionary resource, define the following terms:

Slack: (*adjective*)

1._____

2a._____

3a._____

3b._____

Mighty: (*adjective*)

1._____

2._____

3._____

Desire: (*transitive verb*)

1._____

2a._____

2b.*archaic*:_____

Solemn: (*adjective*)

1._____

2._____

3a._____

3b._____

3c._____

Scripture Study – Zephaniah 3:14-20

Zephaniah was a prophet of God. In this passage, the Lord is making a promise to His people to deliver them from trouble.

1. What does the Lord tell Israel to do in verse 14?

2. According to verse 15, why should Israel be glad?

3. According to verse 16, what does God want Israel to do?

4. According to verse 17, where is the Lord?

5. What is He doing?

6. According to verse 19, what are many of the things that the Lord has promised to do for His people?

7. According to verse 20, what will the Lord do after He gathers His people together?

8. Who was sent by the Father to accomplish salvation for His people?

9. Do you believe that God delivers His people from their enemies?

10. Based on your studies this week, what questions do you have for your parents? Please write them on page 88.

Week 22

Scripture Memory Work: New Testament

"In him was life; and the life was the light of men. And the light shineth in darkness; and the darkness comprehended it not."

-John 1:4-5 (KJV)

Using a Merriam-Webster dictionary resource, define the following terms:

Hope: (*noun*)
1. *archaic*:_____
2a._____
_____
2b._____
_____
2c._____

Want: (*noun*)
1a._____
1b._____
_____
2._____
3._____

Woe: (*noun*)
1._____
_____
2._____

Shame: (*noun*)
1a._____
_____
1b._____
_____
2._____
_____
3a._____
_____
3b._____

Scripture Study – John 1:1-18

1. According to verses 1 & 2, Who was in the beginning with God?

2. According to verse 3, what was made by Him?

3. According to verse 4, what is found in Him?

4. According to verses 6 & 7, for what purpose did John the Baptist come?

5. Was John that light? (verse 8)

6. According to verse 10, did the world know the Word?

7. According to verse 11, did his own receive him?

8. According to verse 12, what do those who believe on Him receive?

9. According to verse 13, how are people **NOT** born again?

10. How **ARE** people born again?

11. According to verse 14, what happened to the Word?

12. Do you know the Word by another Name? What is it?

13. Based on your studies this week, what questions do you have for your parents? Please write them on page 88.

Questions for Parents:

William Kethe (? – 1594)

All People That on Earth Do Dwell

All people that on earth do dwell,
Sing to the Lord with cheerful voice.
Him serve with fear, His praise forth tell;
Come ye before Him and rejoice.

The Lord, ye know, is God indeed;
Without our aid He did us make;
We are His folk, He doth us feed,
And for His sheep He doth us take.

O enter then His gates with praise;
Approach with joy His courts unto;
Praise, laud, and bless His Name always,
For it is seemly so to do.

For why? the Lord our God is good;
His mercy is forever sure;
His truth at all times firmly stood,
And shall from age to age endure.

To Father, Son and Holy Ghost,
The God Whom Heaven and earth adore,
From men and from the angel host
Be praise and glory evermore.

Praise God, from Whom all blessings flow;
Praise Him, all creatures here below;
Praise Him above, ye heavenly host;
Praise Father, Son, and Holy Ghost.

All People That on Earth Do Dwell/Doxology
William Kethe (? – 1594)
"Come ye before Him and rejoice!"

Do you remember the game *"Follow the Leader"*? We have all played that game! All your friends would take turns at leading, and you had to follow them wherever they chose to go. When it was your turn, how well did you lead? Did you often try to make it difficult for those following you? Oftentimes, that is what makes the game fun to play. When you are the leader, you must make many decisions about the direction of the group.

William Kethe had to make many decisions as well. Not much is known of his younger life, but many people believe he was from Scotland because his name is grouped with John Knox, a famous Scottish Reformer. William loved the Psalms, and would write hymns and Psalms that were easy for people to sing. He spent many years in Geneva, Switzerland helping to translate the Geneva Bible. One of William's most famous writings is based in Psalm 100. In that psalm, the writer calls God's children "sheep". Sheep cannot really care for themselves. They are not very independent animals. They cannot fight well. They often get lost when going somewhere. Sheep need someone to care for them. Sheep need a shepherd.

In many passages all through the Bible, God paints pictures of a shepherd and sheep. He called many people who were shepherds to do His work. Abraham, Moses and David were all shepherds. God sent angels to announce Jesus' birth to shepherds out in their fields. Jesus even called Himself the Good Shepherd, Who "lays down His life for the sheep." (John 10:11) You see, if you are God's child, you are playing the most marvelous game of follow the leader! The Bible calls you a sheep, and indeed you are. You do not know all things, but Jesus does. You cannot win the fight against the enemy, but Jesus did and can! You do not know how to fully care for yourself, but Jesus does. You do not know what are the best decisions for your future, but Jesus does.

Another famous psalm that speaks of sheep and shepherds is Psalm 23. It speaks of green pastures and still waters. It tells of how the Lord leads and feeds His sheep. He keeps their enemies at bay. He fills their lives with overflowing joy. He leads them down the right paths for the glory of His name. Even when His sheep walk through darkness and what seems like death, they have nothing to fear. His rod of correction and His staff of guidance are always with them. Every day of their lives is marked by goodness and mercy. They are never lacking any good thing. Doesn't that sound like an amazing game of *"Follow the Leader"*? It is! If you cannot see your life in that light, ask Jesus to give you ears to hear and eyes to see. He is the Rewarder of those that diligently seek Him!

Week 23

Scripture Memory Work: Old Testament

"Know ye that the Lord he is God: it is he that hath made us, and not we ourselves; we are his people, and the sheep of his pasture."

-Psalm 100:3 (KJV)

Using a Merriam-Webster dictionary resource, define the following terms:

Dwell: (*intransitive verb*)

1._____

2a._____

2b._____

3a._____

3b._____

Cheerful: (*adjective*)

1a._____

1b._____

2._____

Approach: (*transitive verb*)

1a._____

1b._____

2a._____

2b._____

Reform: (*transitive verb*)

1a._____

1b._____

2._____

3._____

Scripture Study – Psalm 100

1. What are all the lands commanded to do in Verse 1?

2. Name some examples of a "joyful noise".

3. According to verse 2, how are we to serve the Lord?

4. According to verse 3, what are we to know?

5. What do you think it means to "know that the Lord made us"?

6. Is there anything that does not depend upon God? Why or why not?

7. Do sheep own the shepherd, or does the shepherd own the sheep?

8. What do you think this says about our relationship to God?

9. According to verse 4, what is to be the attitude of our heart?

10. According to verse 5, how long does God's truth endure?

11. Based on your studies this week, what questions do you have for your parents? Please write them on page 96.

Week 24

Scripture Memory Work: New Testament
"I am the good shepherd: the good shepherd giveth his life for the sheep."
-John 10:11 (KJV)

Using a Merriam-Webster dictionary resource, define the following terms:

Hireling: (*noun*)
1._____
_____

Mercenary: (*noun*)
1._____
_____

Abundant: (*adjective*)
1a._____
1b._____
2._____

Destroy: (*verb*)
1._____
_____
_____

2a._____
2b._____
2c._____

Sacrifice: (*verb*)
1._____
2._____
_____
3._____

Scripture Study – John 10:7-14

1. What does Jesus call Himself in verse 7?

2. According to verse 8, what were the people who came before Jesus?

3. Did the sheep hear these people?

4. According to verse 9, what will happen to the people who come to Jesus?

5. According to verse 10, what does the thief come to do?

6. In direct contrast, what does Jesus come to give?

7. According to verses 12 & 13, what does the hireling care more about, money or sheep?

8. Does the hireling own the sheep?

9. Is the hireling brave? Is he a good leader?

10. According to verse 14, who knows the sheep?

11. Do the sheep know the good shepherd?

12. Based on your studies this week, what questions do you have for your parents? Please write them on page 96.

Questions for Parents:

Resources

Bell, Mackenzie. *Christina Rossetti: A Biographical and Critical Study.* Boston: Roberts Brothers, 1898.

Crosby, Fanny. *Fanny Crosby's Life Story.* New York City: Everywhere Publishing Company, 1903.

Dorricott, Rev. I and Rev. T Collins. *Lyric Studies: A Hymnal Guide.* London, Thomas Danks, 1933.

Duffield, Samuel Willoughby. *English Hymns: Their Authors and Their Histories.* New York: Funk and Wagnalls, 1894.

Everett, Grace Morrison. *Hymn Treasures.* Cincinnati: Jennings and Graham, 1905.

Hart, Joseph. *The Lives of British Hymn Writers.* London: Farncombe and Son, 1910.

Hatfield, Edwin F. *The Poets of the Church.* New York: A.D.F. Randolph & Company, 1984.

Lewis, H. Elvet. *Sweet Singers of Wales.* London: The Religious Tract Society, 1933.

Peterson, William J. and Ardythe. *The Complete Book of Hymns.* Carol Stream, Illinois: Tyndale Publishing Co., 2006.

Smith, Jane Stuart with Betty Carlson. *Great Christian Hymn Writers.* Wheaton, Illinois: Crossway Books, 1997.

Wells, Amos R. *A Treasure of Hymns.* Boston and Chicago: United Society of Christian Endeavor, 1914.

www.ingramcontent.com/pod-product-compliance
Lightning Source LLC
Chambersburg PA
CBHW081258170426
43198CB00017B/2835